Hello Mommy

Orangebooks Publication

1st Floor, Rajhans Arcade, Mall Road, Kohka, Bhilai, Chhattisgarh 490020
Website: **www.orangebooks.in**

© Copyright, 2024, Author

All rights reserved. No part of this book may be reproduced, stored in a retrieval system, or transmitted, in any form by any means, electronic, mechanical, magnetic, optical, chemical, manual, photocopying, recording or otherwise, without the prior written consent of its writer.

First Edition, 2024
ISBN: 978-93-6554-333-9

Ravula's...

Hello Mommy

Dr.R venkatagauthamreddy

OrangeBooks Publication
www.orangebooks.in

Acknowledgements

I am deeply grateful to the children and mothers whose stories and experiences have touched my heart and sparked the idea for this book. A special thanks to Dr. K. Akshitha Datta for her meticulous editing, without which this project might have remained unfinished for another year. I am incredibly thankful to Dr. Laxmi, whose generous support helped bring this project to fruition.

I can never thank my family and friends enough for their unwavering love and support through every step of this journey.

You've all made this possible.

ೕ಄ೊ

Foreword

I am grateful for the opportunity to write the preface for the book written by Dr. Gautham, who is a dedicated and sincere professional, passionate about sharing his knowledge on baby care. This book provides valuable insights for mothers, explaining common baby symptoms, such as why babies cry, as well as important practices like burping to prevent aspiration before discharge.

He also highlighted about SIDS(sudden infant death syndrome)and monitors which are sparsely used in India, shared about breast milk values to be followed by mothers.

We hope many families will find this book exciting to read.

Thank you.

- Dr. Laxmi
MBBS, MS Obstetrician and Gynaecologist
Chairman Laxmi Hospitals.

Preface

As soon as a mother is conceived, Parents get a lot of doubts about how to proceed further and once a child is born, families of parents make them rush to hospital many times for trivial problems. This book is designed to address some of the common concerns faced by parents and their families, providing clarity and guidance on caring for their newborn.

享

This information is provided for educational and informational purposes only and does not constitute providing medical advice or professional services. The information provided should not be used for diagnosing or treating a health problem or disease, and those seeking personal medical advice should consult with a licensed physician.

How To Use This Book

While most of the topics discussed here are essential for parents to know, if you're short on time, focus on thoroughly reading the initial chapters on baby care, as they are crucial. For the rest, you can directly search for specific problems as needed.

Contents

Folic Acid Supplementation.. 1

Care After Pregnancy Confirmation 2

    First Visit:..2

Maternal Problems And Effects On Baby.................. 4

Post Birth Baby Care 7

Points Parents Should Know When They
Are Getting Discharged From Hospital...................... 9

    Benefits of Breast Feeds for the Baby 9

    Benefits For Mother 10

    How To Feed The Baby 10

How Will I Know Whether My Baby Is Well 14

Abnormal Baby Will Be Quite Opposite To The
Normal Baby.. 15

General Doubts 17

    1.   Sleep 17

    2.   Oil Massage 17

    3.   Hair 18

    4.   Palms / Hands Are Blues In Color 19

    5.   Shivering In A Baby 19

    6.   Nose 20

7.	Swelling on The Head	20
8.	Teeth	21
9.	Swelling At Nipple & Milk Flow In Baby	21
10.	Urine	21
11.	Bleeding From Vagina In The Baby	22
12.	White Discharge In Baby Girl	22
13.	Skin Rash	23
14.	Peeling Of Skin	23
15.	Blue Spot-On Skin	24
16.	My Baby Is Crying Continuously Or Excessive Cry In Baby	25
17.	Motions	28
a.	Loose Motion:	29
b.	Baby Passes Motion After Feeding:	29
c.	Baby Passing Motion Or Urine By Straining Or By Making Sound:	29
18.	Jaundice & Phototherapy	29
19.	Preterm Care	30
20.	Vaccination Chart	32
21.	Vaccination Doubts	34

Common Baby Care Concerns And Simple Solutions 36

a.	Eyes	36
b.	Mouth	36
c.	Neck Redness And Skin Peeling	36

d.	Peeling Skin In Baby	37
e.	Rapid Breathing & Pauses	37
f.	Hiccups	37
g.	Vomiting In Babies	38
h.	Arching Of Chest And Bending, Fuzzy Baby After Feed	38
i.	Sudden Jerks Of Baby To Sound	38
j.	Baby Butt & Genitals Becoming Red Diaper Rash	39
k.	Urine Dark Yellow	39
l.	Baby Not Gaining Weight	39
m.	Baby Development	39
n.	My Baby Is Putting Everything In Mouth	40
o.	My Baby Is Not Walking And Developing Properly Compared To Other Children	40
p.	My Child Is Not Talking	40
q.	Refusal Of Feeds – My Baby Is Not Feeding Milk	40

Breastfeeding Doubts 42

a.	How Frequently Should The Baby Be Fed	42
b.	Should We Mandatorily Feed The Baby Every 2nd Hour?	42
c.	Duration Of Feed	42
d.	How Long Should I Breastfeed?	43
e.	Bottle Nipple Versus Mother Nipple	43
f.	Should Breastfeeding Be Continued If Mother Is Ill.	44

g.	Can Twins Be Exclusively Breastfeed	44
h.	What Food Mother Should Take While Feeding	44
i.	How can a working mother feed her babies	44
j.	Can a mother with small breast produce enough milk	44
k.	Breastfed babies are leaner than top feed babies	44
l.	Is breastfeeding easier or bottle feeding easier	45
m.	Does breastfeeding make mother breast saggy and unattractive	45
n.	Should breastfeeding be stopped by pregnant mother	45

Complementary Feeding 46

Hello Mommy

Folic Acid Supplementation

Folic acid & its importance - prevents neural tube defects - start before planning pregnancy 400 mcg, remember it is micrograms not milligrams.

Care After Pregnancy Confirmation

(Antenatal Care)

Your obstetrician will focus primarily on the mother's care. This book highlights the essential and crucial aspects related to the baby, ensuring you have the necessary information for your newborn's well-being.

First Visit:

- Measure height and weight.
- Do the important blood tests such as blood grouping, CBP, HIV, Hep-B, blood sugar levels, etc.
- First trimester ultrasound- (In first three months) Where baby is checked for any anatomical defects.

- Iron and calcium supplements need to be taken daily.
- Avoid sleeping on your back after 20 weeks of pregnancy.
- Regular visits as suggested by your gynecologist.

Maternal Problems And Effects On Baby

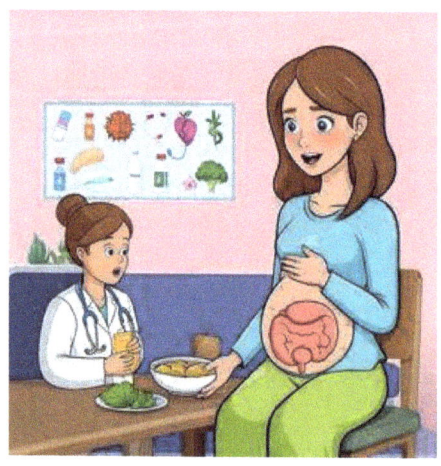

Mothers need to know about some common health issues during pregnancy, as they can affect the baby. Few of the Common problems are discussed here:

Mother's Nutrition: If mother does not take food properly then baby will not grow properly and can cause growth retardation in baby, so highest concentration should be given to the food being taken by mother.

Mothers with Diabetes: If a mother has diabetes, then the baby may develop low blood sugar after birth. It can also cause various defects if mother's diabetes is not kept in control.

Mothers with high Blood Pressure: This can cause growth retardation in the baby, so Blood Pressure of the mothers should be regularly checked throughout pregnancy.

Mother's medications: If mother is taking any medication, this should be informed to the gynecologist as few medicines may affect the unborn child.

Smoking and Drinking during Pregnancy: These should be stopped immediately as they will have dangerous consequences for the unborn child.

Mother's thyroid problem: If a mother develops hypothyroidism during pregnancy, it should be promptly managed, as it can impact the baby. During pregnancy, the mother's thyroid hormone requirements are increased.

Maternal infections: If a mother develops any infection particularly in the first three months, it should be promptly informed to your doctor and treatment needs to be taken immediately. Urinary infection in the last 3 months can cause sepsis in the newborn.

Rupture of membrane: A delay of more than 18 hours between the rupture of the amniotic sac and the delivery of the baby increases the risk of infection for the baby. If any issues arise with your baby, consult your obstetrician and pediatrician promptly.

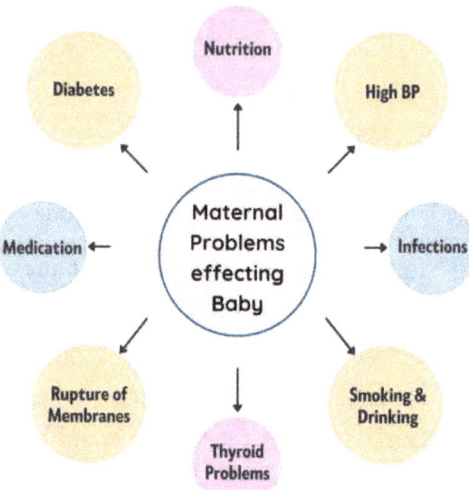

Negative blood group in mother: Your baby has a high chance of developing jaundice, most of the time the first baby will not have any problem.

The second baby will have a higher chance of breakage of red blood cells, jaundice and other complications.

Prevention- Take Anti-D Immunoglobulins, consult your obstetrician.

Post Birth Baby Care

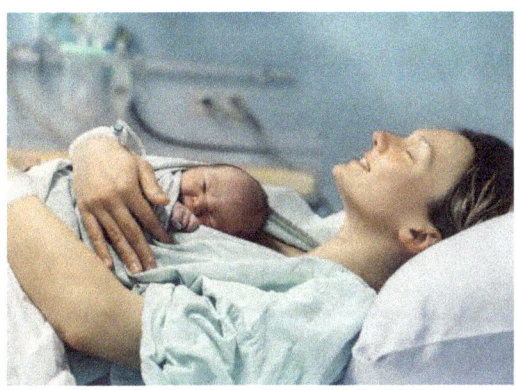

Initiation of breast feeds- Initiate breastfeed as soon as possible, try to establish skin to skin contact of baby with mother.

Keep feeding your baby, as regular feeding stimulates milk production. Please give it a try.

Try to feed the baby every 2nd hourly followed by 10-15 min of burping. (on demand feeding can also be given)

Keep the baby warm by using a head cover, gloves for hands and legs and adequate clothing.

Maintain hygiene, make sure you wash your hands when you touch your baby.

- Avoid overcrowding in hospitals, as it can cause transmission of cold, cough or any other infection to the baby.

- Keep the baby in the same room and bed where mother is present. Keep the baby in a cradle or away only when the mother is sleeping.
- Umbilical cord should be kept dry, fold the nappy below the cord.
- Bath the baby only after the cord falls off & umbilicus is dry, till then sponging can be done.
- Avoid kajal, baby powders, etc.
- Don't give honey or any other feed besides mother's milk to the newborn.

Points Parents Should Know When They Are Getting Discharged From Hospital

Baby should be fed with mother milk for six months compulsory, later you can start complementary feeds.

Benefits of Breast Feeds for the Baby

- Breastfeeding is more convenient compared to formula feeding, as it does not require preparation or strict hygiene practices.
- Breastfeeding is economical as there is no additional cost of purchasing the formula feeds.
- **Colostrum** or first milk of mother on first day needs to be given to the baby, we can consider this as first vaccine.
- Adequate growth of baby's body and brain.

- Reducing the risk of illnesses and the need for repeated hospital admissions as breast milk provides protection against infections

Benefits For Mother

- Decreased chances of breast cancer to mother.
- Less bleeding post-delivery in mother.
- Reduction in the mother's stomach to normal size faster, as the mother's baby sac comes to normal size faster after delivery.
- Early loss of fat gained by mother during pregnancy.

How to feed the baby

1. Support your baby using your hand. So that the baby's head, neck and shoulder rest on your hand.

2. Always keep the baby's head in a higher position.

3. Touch mother's nipple to the angle at baby's mouth & let the baby grasp the nipple and the whole areola (black margin around nipple) is in baby's mouth.

Use one breast at a time for feeding, and ensure it is completely emptied before switching to the other breast. Initially, the milk produced is more watery and helps quench the baby's thirst. Later, the milk becomes thicker and provides essential energy for the baby. Avoid giving the baby half from one breast and half from the other, as this can lead to digestive issues, such as watery stools.

Adequacy of feeds:

Many mothers will get an important doubt whether or not my baby is getting adequate feed?

These points will clear up your doubts:

1. After the baby feeds, the baby becomes playful, or it goes to sleep.

2. Mother feels breast has been emptied.

3. Milk flows on the baby's cheeks when the baby is feeding.

4. Check the urine output; avoid using diapers at home and instead use cloths to tie around the baby. If the baby passes urine six to seven times in 24 hours, it indicates that they are getting adequate feeds, so there's no need to worry.

5. All of these points are not essential but at least a few of them should be present in the mother's mind.

Additional points to be remembered at discharge are:

1. Make sure BCG, Polio, Hep-B are given to your baby. Follow the vaccinations either government or private (IAP) schedules, which ever you feel is convenient, but at any cost vaccinate your child.

2. Give vitamin D for at least 1 year. It should be 400 IU per day. Various brands are available in concentration (See the label/ side of box)

   1 ml usually contains 400 IU or 800 IU.

   If the brand shows 1 ml contain 400 IU then give 1 ml daily of that vit-D brand to the baby

   If the brand shows 1 ml contains 800 IU then gives 0.5 ml daily of that brand vit-D to the baby.

3. Watch for signs of jaundice. If necessary, seek medical advice and consider phototherapy if required.

4. Do a newborn screen and blood grouping after 48 hrs, most of the time your doctor will advise it. At least get a TSH (thyroid screen) if all the newborn screens are not possible for you. You should remember that thyroid problems can occur at any age from newborn baby to adults. If your baby is hypothyroid (means if your baby thyroid level is low) then it will influence your baby's brain development.

5. Do a hearing test BERA at 4 weeks of age if possible.

How Will I Know Whether My Baby Is Well

1. Normal baby will be active- which means it will see, move hands and legs, be playful, cries when hungry or upset.

2. It will generally feed properly most of the time without any trouble.

3. The chest should move slowly and regularly. Occasional hiccups and fast breathing are normal for a baby; don't worry, they will pass.

4. Baby's body will be pink.

5. Body, hands and legs will be warm.

Abnormal Baby Will Be Quite Opposite To The Normal Baby

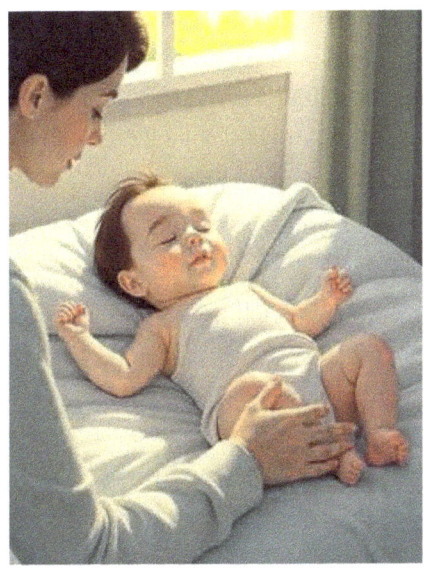

1. It will be dull; it will not move hands and legs properly. If you stimulate, by gently tapping their legs, the baby will be drowsy.

2. Baby will not feed properly, urine output will come down (most important).

3. Rapid breathing and frequent chest movements may indicate an infection in the baby's chest, such as

pneumonia. Unlike occasional fast breathing, this will be persistent.

4. If a baby's body color turns blue, it is a grave sign and should not be ignored. Be very careful and seek immediate medical attention.

5. Do not confuse a baby's entire body turning blue with the hands and feet turning blue (acrocyanosis). Acrocyanosis indicates that the baby is cold and needs warming; it is not a dangerous sign.

    a. Hands, feet and body of baby are cold- baby can be in hypothermia (cover the baby)

    b. If you see any of the above-mentioned problems visit the nearest children's specialist or you can consult me online for any doubts.

General Doubts

1. Sleep

My baby sleeps a lot- yes babies sleep most of the time don't worry. During pregnancy, the baby sleeps in the morning and will be awake at night. After the baby comes out, he may repeat this pattern for a few days.

2. Oil massage

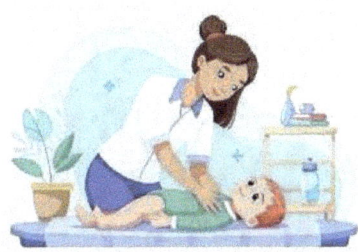

A gentle massage is fine, with vegetable or coconut oil, don't overdo it and fracture the baby. Don't massage the soft area of scalp where there is no bone present.

You can use coconut oil or any good-quality brand oil for baby massage. Massage should be done gently without applying force, as vigorous massage can cause injuries, including fractures. Avoid massaging the baby's head in areas where there is only skin and no bone. When done properly, massage can be a soothing experience for the baby.

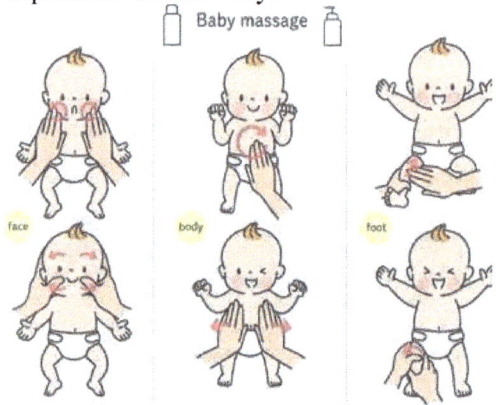

3. Hair

My baby has less hair- don't worry hair will grow. If there is hair loss later, most of the time as the baby's age increases, hair will grow.

4. Palms / hands are blues in color

It is acrocyanosis, it says your baby is not getting adequate heat, cover the baby properly, put gloves on hand, don't panic and don't worry eventually once the baby becomes warm, blue hand color becomes pink.

5. Shivering in a baby

There are various causes for shivering in babies. We call it jitteriness. There are many reasons for it; Few of them are hypothermia (keep the baby warm), hypoglycemia low blood glucose levels (feed the baby)- if the baby is active and feeding well then do the above corrections, before meeting the pediatrician.

6. Nose

Small micro spots on the nose- we call them milia- don't worry they will eventually subside.

7. Swelling on the head

This is seen in normal deliveries and is referred to as caput. It will gradually subside over time. Another type of soft swelling, called cephalohematoma, is less common. It feels softer than caput and also resolves gradually, it can occasionally lead to prolonged jaundice.

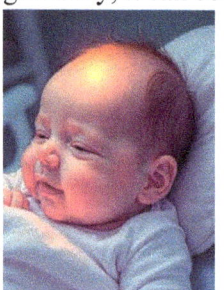 

8. Teeth

If there are teeth, these need to be removed as they may interfere with feeding, see the dentist.

9. Swelling at nipple & milk flow in baby

Don't worry; This are caused by the mother's hormones in the baby and will subside gradually. Do not squeeze or attempt to remove any fluid, as this will resolve on its own.

10. Urine

We can wait 24 to 48 hrs after birth for the baby to pass urine.

Don't get anxious, feed the baby properly, most of the time your baby will pass urine subsequently.

11. Bleeding from vagina in the baby

This may occasionally occur due to the mother's hormones passed down to the baby. Don't worry; it will resolve gradually on its own.

12. White discharge in baby girl

This will subside gradually no need to worry.

13. Skin rash

Most of the time its a normal rash- we call it Erythema toxicum, it will gradually subside by applying coconut oil on the baby.

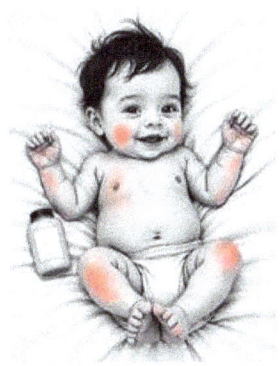

14. Peeling of skin

This occurs sometimes, don't worry apply coconut oil, it will subside gradually.

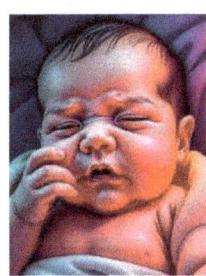
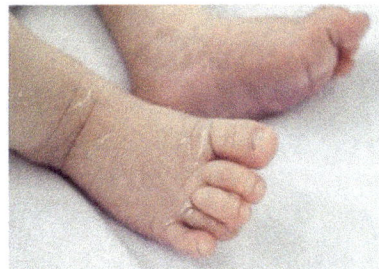

15. Blue spot-on skin

We call this Mongolian spots. They will disappear in a few years don't worry.

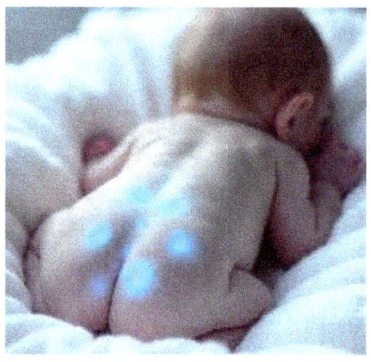

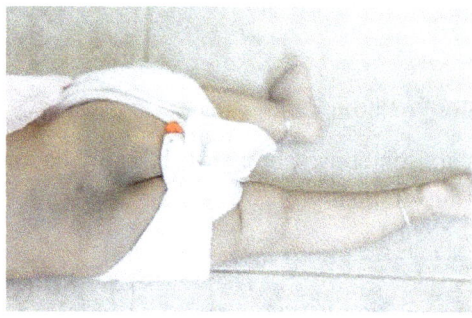

16. My Baby Is Crying Continuously or Excessive Cry in Baby

Sometimes, babies cry excessively or inconsolably, often due to gas or colic pain in their tummy. Occasionally, it could be caused by a mild cold or, rarely, an ear infection.

Kindly follow the following steps if your baby does not stop crying.

> Crying baby

↓

Check the diaper if there is motion and urine in it and change it immediately.

↓

Feed the baby/burp properly. I mean pat the back of the baby so that the gas in the baby's stomach comes out.

↓

baby continues crying

↓

see if anything is irritating the baby such as bet sheet, or check for insect bites

↓ Still crying

Put colic aid drops, 8 drops in baby's mouth

95% babies stop crying here only

(many antispasmodic drops available use any brand colic aid drops is one such brand)

↓

Wait for 15-20 mins.

↓

Still crying

↓

Give nasal saline drops

(Ex. Nasoclear, you can use any brand)

↓

2^0 drops in each nose with gap of 5 min between two nostrils

↓

Still crying

↓

Get otogesic drops

If the baby cries even after the following steps visit the children's specialist or you can consult me online.

17. Motions:

Baby motions

↓

At birth wait for 24 hrs for the baby to pass motion.

↓

Not passing stools

↓

Check thyroid levels consult, children's specialist or me online

1. Later after baby passes the first motion
2. Sometimes mothers may doubt that my baby is not passing motion regularly.

Its normal for babies not to pass motion regularly wait for 3 to 4 days

↓

If babies abdomen is soft and passing gas don't worry

↓

Lastly use glycerine suppository which is safe

a. Loose motion:

In the first 3-5 days, it is normal for the baby to pass frequent motions, known as transitional stools. Don't worry, as this will subside. However, if the stool has a bad smell and is very watery, it may indicate an infection due to poor hygiene. In such cases, consult a pediatrician or feel free to contact me for guidance.

Check if the mother is emptying milk from one breast completely in a feed, as feeding the baby only the initial watery milk from both breasts without fully emptying one can sometimes lead to loose stools..

b. Baby passes motion after feeding:

This is normal for newborn babies we call this gastro colic reflex.

c. Baby passing motion or urine by straining or by making sound:

The abdominal muscles of the baby are not yet fully developed, so they may make noises or strain while passing urine or stool. There's no need to worry; this will improve gradually as the baby grows.

18. Jaundice & phototherapy

My baby eyes and body became yellow:

Most cases of jaundice, known as neonatal hyperbilirubinemia, occur in almost all babies. Consult a pediatrician or me to determine if the levels have crossed the range or threshold. This type of jaundice typically occurs during the first month due to the breakdown of excess blood in the baby's body. Treatment usually involves phototherapy if the bilirubin levels are above the threshold; no unnecessary medications are needed for jaundice. If the levels are below the threshold, the jaundice will naturally subside on its own.

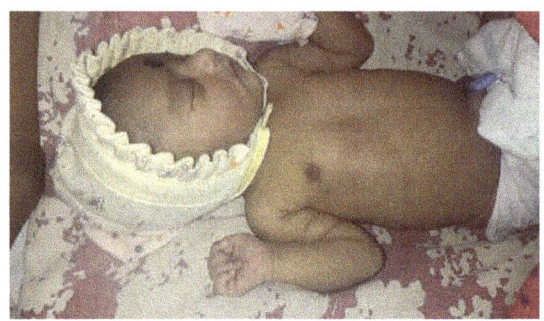

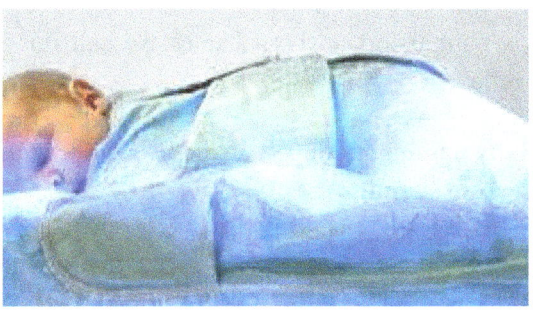

19. Preterm care:

This section is mostly for babies *born before 37 weeks of pregnancy*.

Important aspects

1. If your doctor advises kangaroo mother care, it should be given mandatorily. It ensures proper weight gain and growth of your preterm baby.

2. Eye checkup for retinopathy of prematurity is also very important in the 4th week.

3. If advised, give multivitamins, calcium, and human milk fortification sachets (HMF) properly according to your pediatrician's guidance.

4. Ensure your child's growth and development are progressing well by having regular visits with your pediatrician.

5. If advised by your children specialist, get BERA/ NSG/ 2D echo tests done promptly.

6. Give utmost importance to feeding the child to ensure it is taking feeds properly.

7. Don't forget to vaccinate your child. Most vaccinations should be given after your child crosses 2 kg weight.

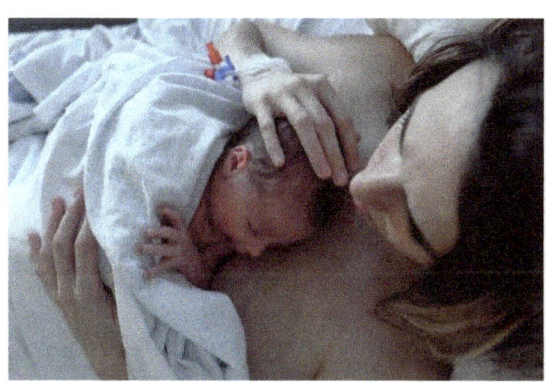

20. Vaccination Chart

Vaccination & Development chart:

Vaccine	Due Date	Given Date	✓ Tick the milestones attained		WL - kg	HL - cm	HC - cm
At birth BCG OPV Hep B - 1 (BD)				• Pull to sit - Newborn complete head lag, back rounded • Ventral suspension - Newborn head sags down • Startle to sound (Do OAE hearing screening)			
6 weeks DTwP/DTaP - 1 Hib - 1 Hep B - 2 PCV - 1 IPV - 1 Rota - 1*				• Momentarily holds the head in horizontal plane • Head control begins • Social : Social smile			
10 weeks DTwP/DTaP - 2 Hib - 2 Hep B - 3 PCV - 2** IPV - 2 Rota - 2				• Responds by smile • Responds to bell • Follows dangling toy at 180 degree • Coos & gurgles • Make eye to eye contact • Turn head towards direction of sound • Begins to recognize the mother's face			
14 weeks DTwP/DTaP - 3 Hib - 3 Hep B - 4 PCV - 3 IPV - 3 Rota - 3				• Pulled to sit, head steady • Prone position, face, head and chest off the Couch • Ventral suspension - head above the plane of trunk • Turns over by 3-5 months • Fine motor: Bi-dexterous approach • Full head control			
6 Months Influenza - 1 6 - 9 months Typhoid TCV 7 Months Influenza - 2				• Prone position - lifts the chin and chest, while supporting weight, on extended arms. • Sits with support (tripod sitting) • Like to look itself in a mirror • Babbles - oh, eh, oo (sounds) • Fine Motor : Transfer objects Holds cube crudely - Uni-dexterous			
9 Months MMR - 1				• Gross motor: Sits well, stands holding on (with support) • Fine motor: immature pincer grasp • Social: waves bye - bye Plays - peek a boo, claps • Language: says bi-syllables (mama, baba, dada) • Look for hidden toys • Respond to name being called			

Hello Mommy

Age	Vaccines	Milestones
1 year	Hepatitis A	• Stands without support • Walks alone, but falls • Mature pincer grasp • Plays simple ball game • 2 words with meaning • Points an object with one finger • Respond to simple request No, come here
15 months	MMR - 2 Varicella 1 PCV booster	• Walks alone • Crawls upstairs • Imitates as taking by phone • Brings and Shows Toys of interest • Tower of 2 cubes
18 months	DTwP - B1/ DTaP - B1 IPV - B1 Hib - B1 Hep - A 2 (Inactivated) varicella - 2	• Runs, explores table drawers • Domestic mimicry • 8-10 words • Throws a ball without falling • Recognizes parts of the body • Tower of 4 cubes • Name and identify common objects in the picture book • Puts pebbles, small objects in a container
2 years	Influenza vaccine	• Walks up and down stairs (2feet/step) • Tower of 6 cubes • Pulls people to show desired object • Two-word Sentences • Able to do two step command
3 years	Influenza vaccine	• Rides tricycle • Alternates feet going upstairs, • 3 word sentences • Tower of 8 cubes, making a Bridge / Gate of 3 cubes • Copies a circle • Knows name & gender • Identify 1 - 2 colours and shapes • Able to do three step command
4 years	Influenza vaccine	• Hops on one foot • Alternates feet going downstairs • Copies cross & square • Steps of 6 cubes • Group play • Says poem, Able to tell A B C D, 1 2 3 4 letters & Simple Story
5 years	DTwP / DTaP - B2 IPV - B2, MMR - 3 Influenza vaccine	• Plays skipping rope • Copies a triangle • Steps of 10 cubes • Count up to 10 • Social : Dresses and undresses • Language : asks for meaning of words • Identify & write letter A B C D, 1 2 3 4 • Identifies 4 colours
9-14 years Tdap & HPV	• T dap : 10-12 y followed by Td every 10 y • HPV : 9-14 years 2 doses 0, 6-12m (2 doses at 6 months interval) >15 years - 3 doses -HPV 0-1-6 mo for HPV2, 0-2-6 mo for HPV4	

Ref IAP - ACVIP Recommendations 2020-21
Blue : Vaccines provided for all Children in the Government set-up.
Red : Vaccines recommended in private practice, for all Children (IAP Recommendations).

21. Vaccination doubts:

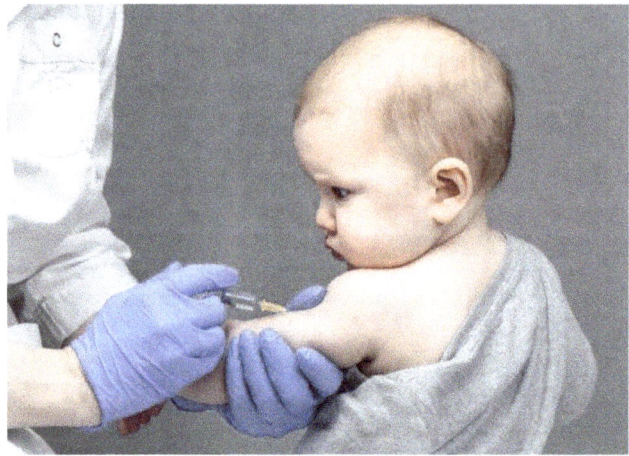

1. Should I vaccinate my child? Yes, vaccination is mandatory for your child.

2. Will my child get a fever with vaccination? Rarely a child can get fever, but that should not stop you from vaccinating your child as it saves your child from dangerous diseases.

3. Government or private vaccination? Go for vaccination whichever you feel more comfortable with and can complete consistently.

4. If you are following the govt schedule- try to vaccinate the pending vaccines (IAP schedule) in the private sector.

5. I skipped a dose of vaccination! Don't worry, your child's specialist will advise on when it can be retaken.

6. My child has a fever now. Can I vaccinate my child? Better avoid vaccination if your child has fever, give the vaccine after your child recovers from fever.

7. Vaccination swelling & redness: Most of the time, the swelling at the vaccination site will subside on its own gradually. In some cases, swelling may persist for a few months, but rubbing the area gently after the vaccine is administered can help minimize this problem.

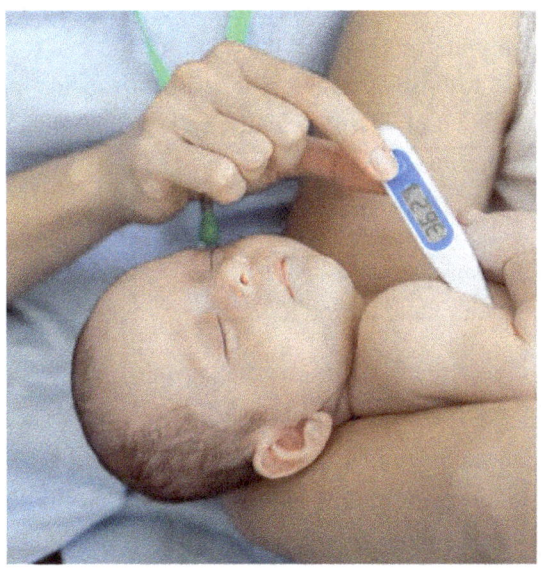

Common Baby Care Concerns And Simple Solutions

a. Eyes

Children may get tears in the early stage if there is obstruction to the tear tube in the eye. Wash your hand thoroughly and massage at the angle of the eye for 5 to 10 min, 4 to 5 times a day. If it does not subside after 1 month, meet a children specialist or you can contact me for consultation.

b. Mouth

Wash the mouth of the baby during the morning after washing your hand thoroughly- it can prevent oral fungal infection.

c. Neck redness and skin peeling

This can some time's occur as mothers tend to forget cleaning the neck after feeding the baby, as the baby's neck is small, there is a chance that milk can go into the folds of baby's neck and cause infection. Try to keep baby's neck dry, use baby powder wait for 3-4 days if it does not subside or worsen, consult a children's specialist or consult me online.

d. Peeling skin in baby

This can sometimes happen, but there's no need to worry. Applying coconut oil or any baby oil will typically help improve the condition within 2 to 3 days.

e. Rapid breathing & pauses

Sometimes babies breathe fast and gradually breathing comes to normal. We call this periodic breathing & this is normal, don't worry. We need to worry only if the breathing of the baby is fast for a longer period, if the baby becomes dull or the baby has chest retractions. (Indrawing of chest)

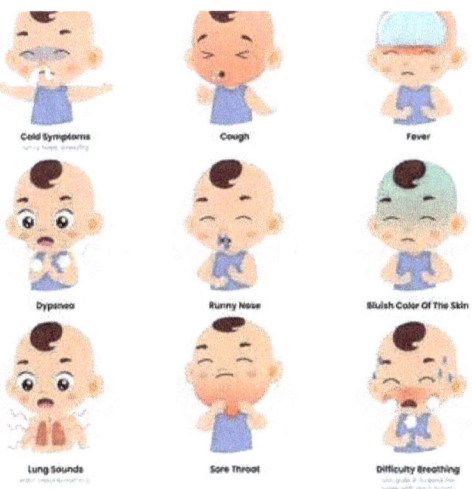

f. Hiccups

Some babies may have hiccups don't worry most of the time they subside on their own.

g. Vomiting in babies

Babies vomit occasionally if burping is not done properly, don't worry. If it is more frequent and if the baby vomits after feeding and placing on bed it can be GERD (weak sphincter or door above the stomach) it will subside most of the time as the baby grows, put the baby in head up position, with legs slanting down using bed sheets when baby sleeps. use the correct position for feeding with the head on the higher side, for such babies do burping for a longer period. If the baby vomits, turn the baby to the left side and clear the vomit, if they become very frequent consult any children's specialist.

h. Arching of chest and bending, fuzzy baby after feed

This also a sign of GERD- use the same precautions mentioned above, most of the time it will subside as the baby grows.

i. Sudden jerks of baby to sound

This is normal in a baby, will be fine after the movement; we call this startle reflex. It is also an indication your baby's ears are working properly, better avoid loud noises near the baby.

j. Baby butt& genitals becoming red- Diaper Rash

It occurs when baby's diapers are not changed when required, that is when the baby passes urine or motion. Don't use diapers when a baby stays at home to prevent this, you can use baby tying cloth instead of diapers when at home. If diaper rash occurs, keep the baby dry, most of the time it will subside on its own, you can also use zinc oxide cream for example siloderm cream morning and night for 5 to 6 days, if it doesn't subsid or worsens, meet the pediatrician or consult me online.

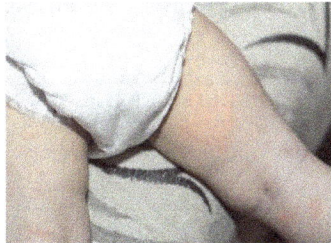

k. Urine dark yellow

Baby is not getting adequate mother feeds, try feeding the baby properly.

l. Baby not gaining weight

Check the adequacy of the mother's milk supply and feed the baby frequently. If needed, wake the baby to ensure they are feeding properly. Monitoring the baby's urine output- there should be 7 to 8 wet diapers per day if the feeding is adequate.

m. Baby development

Mother and father need to interact with the baby, they need to give time for the baby to grow and develop properly.

n. My baby is putting everything in mouth

This shows your baby is developing properly. That is one of the ways babies explore the surrounding environment, babies are not doing this due to teething (it's a misconception). Our job as parents is to keep the floor and baby toys clean by washing at least every 3 to 5 days, otherwise there is a chance your baby can develop motions and vomitings.

o. My baby is not walking and developing properly compared to other children

Most of the time, you may need to consult a children's specialist who can check if there are any concerns with the baby. After basic tests and evaluations, if the children's specialist assures you that everything is fine, there's no need to worry. Not all children will develop milestones at the same pace; some may develop a bit faster while others may be slightly slower. Ensure there are no significant differences in your baby's development compared to other children. Ultimately, most children will achieve all their developmental milestones.

p. My child is not talking

If the child responds to sounds and is active, and other milestones have been properly achieved, there's no need to worry. The child may start speaking a few months later, but they will ultimately speak. Sometimes speech development can be delayed in nuclear families, especially when children spend time with only adults or are not exposed to peers of the same age who speak. Parents should interact more with their child and encourage verbal communication. This is more common in families with working parents and those with a more isolated family structure. Follow these tips, and your child will speak eventually.

q. Refusal of feeds- my baby is not feeding milk

Check weather your child is having cold, sometimes nasal block can cause this problem, putting saline drops in the nose (any brand) is fine, examples of brands: nasoclear, active cold drops.

Breastfeeding Doubts

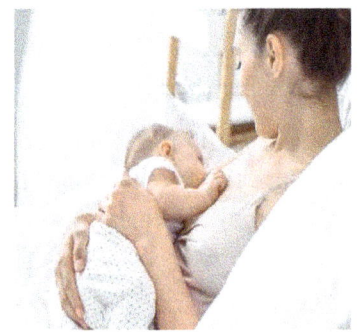

a. How frequently should the baby be fed

Most newborn babies like to feed every 2 to 3 hours, nighttime feeding also should be done.

b. Should we mandatorily feed the baby every 2nd hour?

A few hours on either side (early or late) is fine—it's not a strict rule or mandatory. You can also follow on-demand feeding. Most babies tend to wake up and feed around the 2nd or 3rd hour. However, if it has been more than 4 hours, it is advisable to wake the baby to feed.

c. Duration of feed

15 to 20 min…. burping should be done properly.

d. How long should I breastfeed?

First 6 months only breastfeeding should be done, not even water is required by the baby. Continue breast feeding for 1 year along with complementary feeds. After 1 year focus should be on solid food with less focus on breastfeed. If milk and breastfeed are given more after 1 year, babies or children tend to have lower weight and some are malnourished.

e. Bottle nipple versus mother nipple

Babies will develop nipple confusion if you offer both bottle nipple and mother nipple, though they appear similar there is a lot of difference. Bottle nipple is easy to suck and get the milk but baby has to work hard to suck from mother nipple. If babies get used to bottle nipple they quickly try to avoid sucking at the mother's nipple. Avoid bottle feed.

f. Should breastfeeding be continued if mother is ill

Breast feeding can be continued even if mother is ill, if mother is having any respiratory illness, she can continue feeding with a mask.

g. Can twins be exclusively breastfeed

Yes, twins can also be given only mother's milk, provided the mother should get adequate nutrition to herself, offer one twin each breast, close monitoring should be kept on weight and development of twins.

h. What food mother should take while feeding

Mother can take all kinds of food during breastfeeding.

i. How can a working mother feed her babies

She has to feed the baby before leaving for work and mother should leave her milk in the house, by using a breast pump or manually squeezing out the milk for the baby. The milk can be safely stored for 8 hours at room temperature and upto 24 hours in refrigerator, use palady to feed the baby.

j. Can a mother with small breast produce enough milk

Breast size does not depend on the quantity of milk produced, don't worry the milk produced by smaller breasts will also have the final quantity produced by regular sized breasts.

k. Breastfed babies are leaner than top feed babies

Breastfeeding is advantageous over formula feeding as the formula fed babies have high risk for developing obesity and diabetes in later stages of life.

l. Is breastfeeding easier or bottle feeding easier

Breastfeeding is generally easier compared to bottle feeding. Using too much water in formula can lead to loose stools in the baby, while insufficient water can cause constipation. Accurate measurement and proper cleanliness of the bottle are crucial for bottle-feeding. Breastfed babies benefit from the transfer of immunity from the mother through her milk, which reduces their risk of developing diseases and often results in fewer hospital admissions.

m. Does breastfeeding make mother breast saggy and unattractive

Not breastfeeding but pregnancy directly will have an effect on shape, size and firmness of breast. Regular exercises of the chest maintains the shape and contour of the breast. Other factors such as excessive weight gain during pregnancy and increasing age also contribute to changes in breast appearance, not breastfeeding itself.

n. Should breastfeeding be stopped by pregnant mother

Continue breast feeding till the other baby reaches atleast 4 months of age, later better avoid it as it can affect nutritional status of the fetus and it will also put more burden on the mother . It is adviced to have a gap of 3 years between babies.

Complementary Feeding

After six months of exclusive breastfeeding start solids gradually, use rice first by mashing it properly. Initially, make the baby's food like a thin soup, allowing them to become accustomed to solid foods. Gradually, as the baby gets used to it, increase the thickness so that the food sticks to the spoon when feeding. After about a month, introduce four or five varieties of dal, mash them well with the rice, and feed the baby. You can start Fruits like banana, mash it properly and give it once the baby gets used to the above feeds for two or three months. Then, include other foods like mashed potato, mashed or grinded carrot, boiled apple etc. Continue offering soft, well-mashed or grinded foods until the child is around 2 years old.

Avoid all packed baby foods as they contain lots of sugar. Don't give any processed food to the baby or children.

Sudden Infant Death Syndrome(SIDS): A rare but dangerous complication causing sudden death of infant can occur rarely in infant, it can occur due to many causes, common one being babies forgetting to take breath. To reduce the risk, avoid placing the baby in a prone position when sleeping- meaning they should not be put down with their face facing the bed and special devices are available in market called SIDS monitors which you can purchase and use for added safety.

Hello Mommy

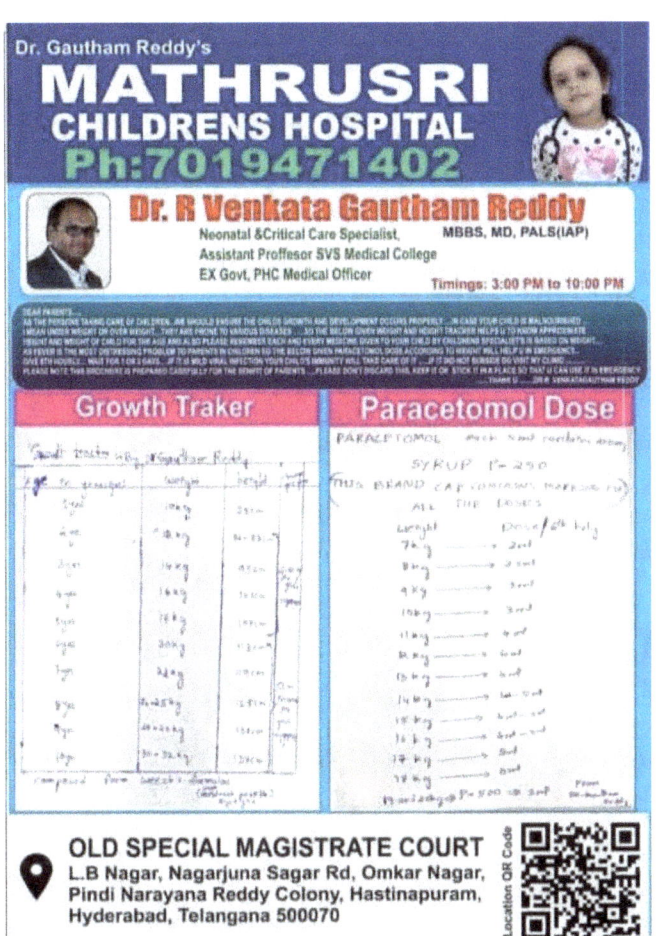

www.ingramcontent.com/pod-product-compliance
Lightning Source LLC
LaVergne TN
LVHW020419070526
838199LV00055B/3672